MASTERING TA
BEADING:

A Comprehensive Guide to Intricate Embellishment

WALTER E. MATHIEU

COPYRIGHT

Table of contents

CHAPTER 1
  Definition
  APPLICATION
  MATERIALS/TOOLS
CHAPTER 2
  Basic Techniques
  Setting Up the Tambour Frame
  Threading the Tambour Hook
  Creating Chain Stitches
  Attaching Beads
  Securing Threads
CHAPTER 3
  Intermediate Techniques
  Picot Stitch
  Layering Beads
  Sequin Attachment
  Combining Embroidery Stitches
  Creating Texture and Dimension
CHAPTER 4

Advanced Techniques

Layering Beads for Dimension

Incorporating Raised Stitches

Mixing Embroidery Stitches

Creating 3D Effects with Beads

Intricate Overlay Techniques

TIPS AND SUCCESS

CHAPTER 5

Beginner Project

Beaded Bracelet

Beaded Flower Brooch

Beaded Bookmark

Beaded Coin Purse

Beaded Hair Accessory

INTERMEDIATE PROJECT

Beaded Clutch Purse

Beaded Evening Shawl

Beaded Statement Necklace

Beaded Decorative Pillow Cover

Beaded Bridal Veil

CHAPTER 6

Advanced Project

Beaded Evening Gown

Beaded Wall Hanging Tapestry

Beaded Bridal Tiara

Beaded Statement Earrings

Beaded Decorative Table Runner

TROUBLESHOOTING AND
SOLUTIONS

CHAPTER 7

Conclusion

INTRODUCTION TO TAMBOUR BEADING

Tambour beading has its origins in India and was introduced to Europe in the 18th century. The technique originated in the region of Kashmir, where skilled artisans used a small, sharp hook attached to a handle to create intricate chain stitches on fabric. This method allowed for the precise attachment of beads and sequins to fabric, resulting in elaborate and finely detailed designs.

Tambour embroidery, which encompasses both beading and stitching, gained popularity in Europe during the 18th and 19th centuries, particularly in France. It became associated with luxury and high fashion, with tambour-embellished garments being coveted by royalty and the aristocracy.

The term "tambour" is derived from the French word for "drum," referring to the drum-like frame used to stretch the fabric during the embroidery process. Over time, tambour beading evolved and spread to other parts of the world, becoming a cherished technique in the realms of fashion, costume design, and textile artistry. Today, tambour beading continues to be admired for its intricate beauty and remains an integral part of the global embroidery tradition.

CHAPTER 1

Definition

Tambour beading is a technique of embellishing fabric with beads, sequins, and other decorative elements using a special hook and frame known as a tambour frame. The process involves creating a series of chain stitches on the fabric, through which beads or sequins are attached, resulting in intricate and elaborate designs. This technique is commonly used in haute couture fashion, bridal wear, and costume design to add texture, sparkle, and dimension to garments and accessories.

APPLICATION

Tambour beading finds application in various fields, including:

1. **Fashion Design:** Tambour beading is extensively used in haute couture fashion to embellish evening gowns, bridal dresses, and couture garments. Designers incorporate tambour beading to add luxury, texture, and intricate detailing to their creations.

2. **Costume Design**: Tambour beading is a staple technique in costume design for theater, film, and television productions. Costumers use tambour beading to create elaborate costumes for characters, adding authenticity and visual interest to period pieces and fantasy ensembles.

3. **Bridal Wear**: Tambour beading is popularly employed in bridal wear to adorn wedding dresses, veils, and

accessories such as belts, sashes, and headpieces. The shimmering effect of beads and sequins enhances the bridal ensemble, providing a touch of elegance and glamour.

4. **Accessories:** Tambour beading is utilized to embellish a wide range of accessories, including handbags, shoes, hats, and jewelry. These embellished accessories add a unique and sophisticated flair to any outfit, making them ideal for special occasions and formal events.

5. **Home Decor:** Tambour beading can also be applied to home décor items such as throw pillows, table runners, curtains, and wall hangings. These embellished home accents can elevate the aesthetic of interior spaces, adding a touch of opulence and personality to any room.

Overall, tambour beading is a versatile technique that allows for creative expression across various fields, enabling artisans and designers to transform fabric into works of art through intricate beadwork and embellishment.

MATERIALS/TOOLS

To embark on tambour beading, you'll need the following materials and tools:

1. **Tambour Frame**: A tambour frame, also known as an embroidery hoop, is essential for holding the fabric taut while you work. It typically consists of two round or oval hoops

that can be adjusted to stretch the fabric evenly.

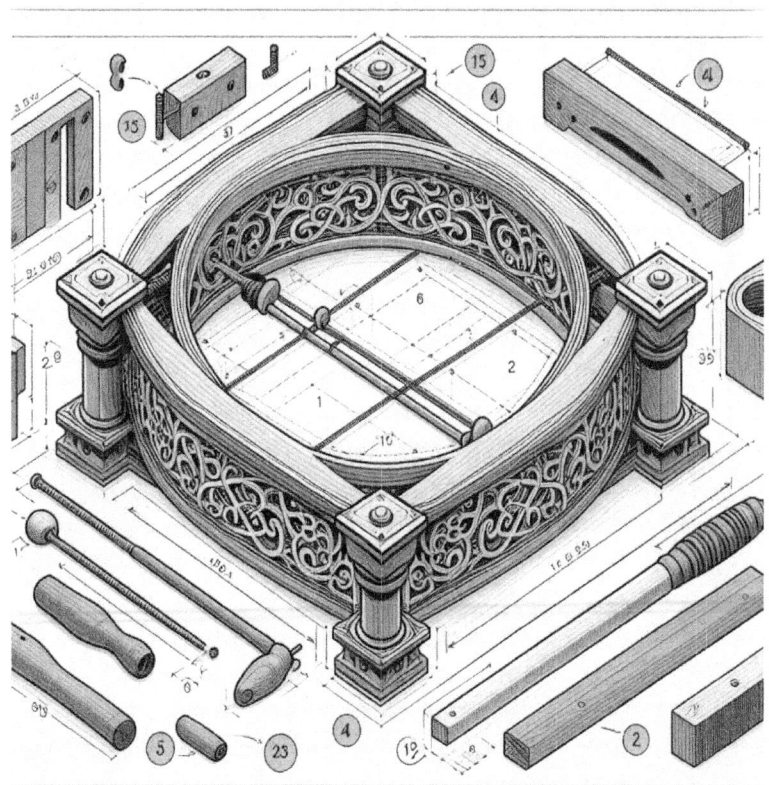

2. **Tambour Hook:** The tambour hook is the primary tool used for creating stitches and attaching beads and sequins to the fabric. It resembles a small, slender crochet hook with a pointed tip, allowing for precise stitching.

3. **Fabric:** Choose a suitable fabric for tambour beading, such as fine silk,

chiffon, tulle, or organza. The fabric should be stable enough to support the weight of beads and sequins without stretching excessively.

4. **Threads**: Use fine embroidery threads or specialized tambour threads that match the color of your fabric. These threads will be used to create the foundation stitches and secure the beads and sequins in place.

5. **Beads and Sequins:** Select beads, sequins, and other decorative elements in various sizes, shapes, and colors to achieve the desired design. Be sure to choose beads with pre-drilled holes that are compatible with your tambour hook.

6. **Thimble:** A thimble can protect your finger from the repetitive motion of pushing the tambour hook through

the fabric, especially when working
with dense beadwork.

7. **Scissors:** Keep a pair of sharp scissors handy for cutting threads and trimming excess fabric.

8. **Magnifier:** Optionally, a magnifying glass or magnifying lamp can aid in working with fine details and intricate designs, especially for those with vision difficulties.

With these materials and tools at hand, you'll be ready to embark on your tambour beading journey and create stunning embellishments with precision and skill.

CHAPTER 2

Basic Techniques

Setting Up the Tambour Frame

- **Materials Needed:** Tambour frame, fabric (silk, chiffon, tulle, etc.)

- **Steps:**

  1. Loosen the screws on the tambour frame to separate the inner and outer hoops.

  2. Place the fabric over the inner hoop, ensuring it is smooth and wrinkle-free.

  3. Position the outer hoop over the fabric and inner hoop, aligning the screws.

  4. Tighten the screws to secure the fabric between the hoops, ensuring it is stretched taut.

Threading the Tambour Hook

- **Materials Needed:** Tambour hook, embroidery thread or tambour thread

- **Steps:**

  1. Thread the tambour hook with a length of embroidery thread or tambour thread.

  2. Insert the threaded hook through the fabric from the back to the front, leaving a tail of thread on the underside.

  3. Pull the tail of thread through to the front, leaving a small loop on the surface of the fabric.

  4. Hold the loop with your non-dominant hand while working the hook with your dominant hand.

Creating Chain Stitches

- **Materials Needed:** Fabric mounted on the tambour frame, threaded tambour hook

- **Steps:**

  1. Insert the hook through the fabric from front to back, catching the loop of thread on the surface.

  2. Rotate the hook so that the pointed end faces upward and grasp the working thread with the hook.

  3. Pull the hook back through the fabric, forming a chain stitch on the surface.

  4. Continue creating chain stitches in a straight line or along a

curved path, adjusting the tension as needed.

Attaching Beads

- **Materials Needed:** Beads (with pre-drilled holes), threaded tambour hook, embroidery or tambour thread

- **Steps:**

  1. Thread a bead onto the tambour hook, sliding it down to the fabric.

  2. Insert the hook through the fabric from front to back, catching the working thread in the process.

  3. Hold the bead in place with your non-dominant hand as you pull the hook back through the fabric.

  4. Continue attaching beads in desired patterns or sequences, spacing them evenly along the chain stitches.

Securing Threads

- **Materials Needed:** Threaded tambour hook,embroidery or tambour thread

- **Steps**:

  1. After completing a section of tambour beading, bring the working thread to the back of the fabric.

  2. Insert the hook through the fabric from front to back, catching the working thread.

  3. Pull the hook through to the back, forming a loop on the surface.

  4. Pass the hook through the loop to create a knot, then trim any excess thread close to the fabric.

By mastering these basic techniques and practicing with different patterns and bead arrangements, you can create beautiful tambour beading designs with precision and skill.

CHAPTER 3

Intermediate Techniques

Picot Stitch

- **Materials Needed:** Fabric mounted on the tambour frame, threaded tambour hook, embroidery or tambour thread, Beads (optional)

- **Stepes**:

  1. Start with a chain stitch on the fabric.

  2. Insert the hook through the fabric from front to back, catching the working thread.

  3. Rotate the hook to face upward and grasp the working thread with the hook.

  4. Pull the hook back through the fabric, forming a loop on the surface.

5. Before pulling the loop tight, slide a bead onto the thread (optional).

6. Pull the loop tight to create a small loop (picot) on the surface.

7. Continue with chain stitches, incorporating picot stitches at regular intervals.

Layering Beads

- **Materials Needed**: Fabric mounted on the tambour frame, threaded tambour hook, embroidery or tambour thread, beads of different sizes and shapes

- **Steps:**

  1. Work a base row of chain stitches on the fabric.

  2. Select a larger bead and thread it onto the tambour hook.

  3. Insert the hook through the fabric from front to back, catching the working thread.

  4. Hold the bead in place with your non-dominant hand as you pull the hook back through the fabric.

  5. Repeat the process with smaller beads, layering them on top of the larger bead to create dimension and texture.

6. Continue layering beads in desired patterns or arrangements, spacing them evenly along the chain stitches.

Sequin Attachment

●**Materials Needed**: Fabric mounted on the tambour frame, threaded tambour hook, embroidery or tambour thread, sequins with center holes

● **Steps:**

1. Thread a sequin onto the tambour hook, ensuring it sits flat against the fabric.

2. Insert the hook through the fabric from front to back, catching the working thread.

3. Hold the sequin in place with your non-dominant hand as you pull the hook back through the fabric.

4. Continue attaching sequins in desired patterns or sequences, spacing them evenly along the chain stitches.

Combining Embroidery Stitches

- **Materials Needed:** Fabric mounted on the tambour frame, threaded tambour hook, embroidery or tambour thread, embroidery needle (optional)

- **Steps:**

  1. Work a base row of chain stitches on the fabric.

  2. Use traditional embroidery stitches such as satin stitch, French knots, or feather stitch to embellish the tambour beading design.

  3. Thread an embroidery needle with matching thread and work the desired embroidery stitches over the tambour beading, integrating them seamlessly into the design.

  4. Experiment with different combinations of tambour beading

and embroidery stitches to create unique and intricate designs.

Creating Texture and Dimension

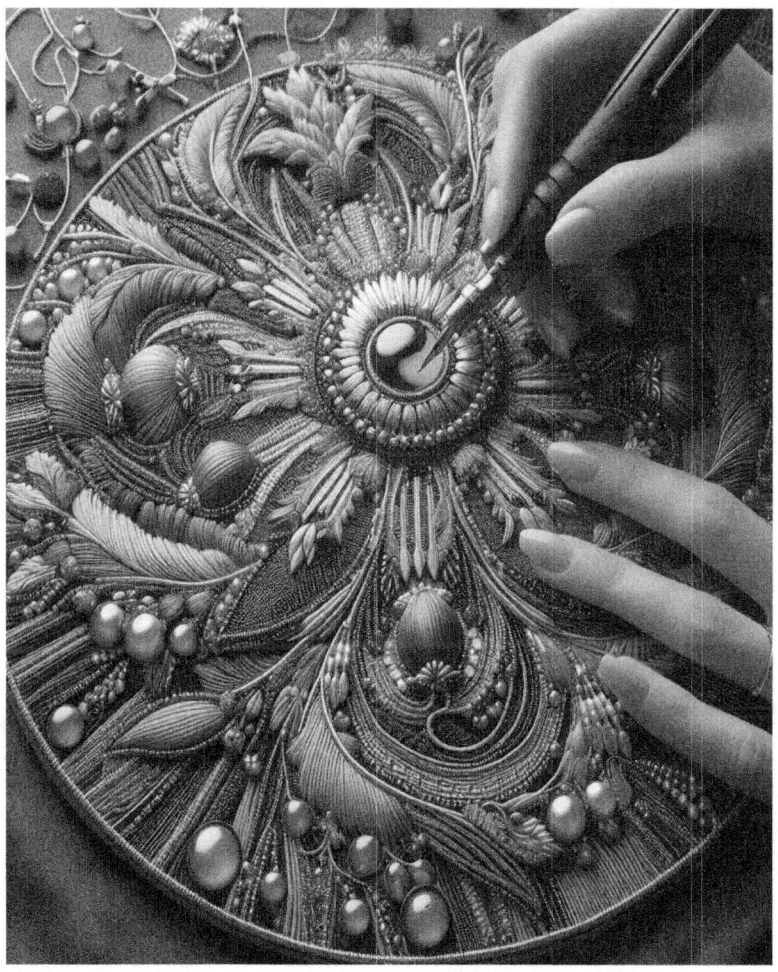

- **Materials Needed:** Fabric mounted on the tambour frame, threaded tambour hook, embroidery or tambour thread, beads, sequins, and other embellishments

- **Steps:**

  1. Experiment with different bead sizes, shapes, and placement to create texture and dimension in your tambour beading design.

  2. Layer beads and sequins to add depth and interest to the surface of the fabric.

  3. Incorporate techniques such as raised stitches, couching, or padding to elevate certain elements of the design.

  4. Play with light and shadow by varying the density and

arrangement of beads and sequins.

By mastering these intermediate techniques, you can elevate your tambour beading skills and create intricate and visually stunning designs with depth, texture, and dimension.

CHAPTER 4

Advanced Techniques

Layering Beads for Dimension

- **Materials Needed: Fabric** mounted on the tambour frame, threaded tambour hook, embroidery or tambour thread, beads of different sizes and shapes

- **Steps:**

  1. Work a base row of chain stitches on the fabric.

  2. Select a larger bead and thread it onto the tambour hook.

  3. Insert the hook through the fabric from front to back, catching the working thread.

  4. Hold the bead in place with your non-dominant hand as you pull the hook back through the fabric.

5. Repeat the process with smaller beads, layering them on top of the larger bead to create dimension and texture.

6. Experiment with different bead combinations and layering techniques to achieve a three-dimensional effect.

Incorporating Raised Stitches

- **Materials Needed:** Fabric mounted on the tambour frame, threaded tambour hook, embroidery or tambour thread

- **Steps:**

  1. Work a base row of chain stitches on the fabric.

  2. Select an area where you want to create a raised effect and mark the outline of the shape.

  3. Use the tambour hook to work rows of closely spaced chain stitches within the outlined shape, stacking them on top of each other.

  4. Gradually increase the tension of the stitches to build height and create a raised effect.

  5. Fill in the outlined shape with additional rows of raised stitches,

alternating the direction of the stitches for added texture and dimension.

Mixing Embroidery Stitches

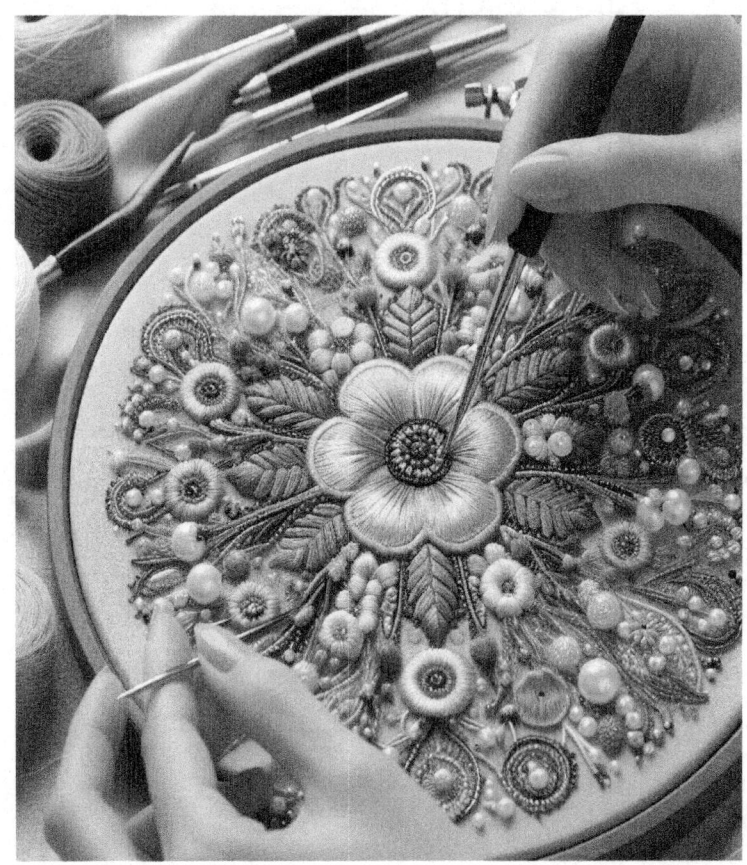

- **Materials Needed:** Fabric mounted on the tambour frame, threaded tambour hook, embroidery or tambour thread, embroidery needles

- **Steps:**

  1. Work a base row of chain stitches on the fabric.

  2. Use traditional embroidery stitches such as satin stitch, French knots, or feather stitch to embellish the tambour beading design.

  3. Thread an embroidery needle with matching thread and work the desired embroidery stitches over the tambour beading, integrating them seamlessly into the design.

  4. Experiment with different combinations of tambour beading

and embroidery stitches to create unique and intricate designs.

5. Use tambour beading as a base to add additional texture and dimension with embroidery stitches, enhancing the overall visual impact of the design.

Creating 3D Effects with Beads

• **Materials Needed:** Fabric mounted on the tambour frame, threaded tambour hook, embroidery or tambour thread, Beads of various shapes and sizes

- **Steps:**

  1. Work a base row of chain stitches on the fabric.

  2. Select beads of different shapes and sizes to create three-dimensional effects.

  3. Experiment with techniques such as stacking beads, layering them at different angles, or creating clusters to mimic natural textures and forms.

  4. Use beads strategically to highlight specific elements of the design, such as flower petals, leaves, or geometric shapes.

  5. Play with light and shadow by varying the placement and density of beads, enhancing the depth and dimensionality of the tambour beading design.

Intricate Overlay Techniques

- **Materials Needed:** Fabric mounted on the tambour frame, threaded tambour hook, embroidery or tambour thread, beads, sequins, and other embellishments

- **Steps**:

  1. Work a base layer of tambour beading on the fabric, using chain stitches or other basic techniques.

  2. Select additional embellishments such as beads, sequins, or metallic threads to create intricate overlays.

  3. Experiment with techniques such as couching, where larger embellishments are attached to the fabric with smaller stitches, or appliqué, where fabric shapes are layered and stitched onto the surface.

  4. Incorporate overlay techniques to add depth, texture, and visual

interest to the tambour beading design, creating a rich and complex surface texture.

5. Pay attention to the placement and arrangement of overlay elements, ensuring they enhance the overall composition and balance of the design.

By mastering these advanced techniques, you can take your tambour beading skills to the next level, creating intricate and visually stunning designs with depth, texture, and dimension.

TIPS AND SUCCESS

Mastering tambour beading requires practice, patience, and attention to detail. Here are some tips to help you succeed in tambour beading:

1. Start with the Basics: Begin by mastering fundamental techniques such as chain stitching and bead attachment before moving on to more advanced techniques. Practice these basic stitches until you feel comfortable with the movements and tension control.

2. Use Quality Materials: Invest in high-quality materials such as fine fabrics, sturdy tambour frames, and sharp tambour hooks. Quality materials will make the process smoother and more enjoyable, and they will also ensure the longevity of your finished pieces.

3. **Practice Consistently**: Like any skill, tambour beading improves with practice. Set aside regular time for practice sessions, even if it's just for a few minutes each day. Regular practice will improve your technique and develop muscle memory.

4. **Experiment with Designs:** Don't be afraid to experiment with different bead sizes, shapes, colors, and placement techniques. Try out various patterns, motifs, and compositions to discover what works best for your style and preferences.

5. **Work in Good Lighting:** Adequate lighting is essential for tambour beading, especially when working with small beads and intricate designs. Make sure you have sufficient natural

or artificial light to see your work clearly and avoid eye strain.

6. Maintain Proper Tension: Consistent tension is crucial for achieving neat and uniform stitches in tambour beading. Avoid pulling the thread too tightly or too loosely, as this can distort the fabric or create uneven stitches. Practice adjusting the tension of your stitches until you find the right balance.

7. Take Breaks: Tambour beading can be a repetitive and intricate process, so it's essential to take breaks to rest your eyes and hands. Stretching, taking short walks, or practicing relaxation techniques can help prevent fatigue and maintain focus.

8. Troubleshoot Problems: If you encounter difficulties such as tangled threads, broken beads, or uneven stitches, don't get discouraged. Take a step back, assess the problem, and try to identify the cause. Consult tutorials, books, or online resources for troubleshooting tips and solutions.

9. Join a Community: Connect with fellow tambour beaders through online forums, social media groups, or local workshops. Sharing tips, techniques, and experiences with others in the community can provide inspiration, motivation, and valuable insights.

10. Celebrate Progress: Remember that tambour beading is a journey, and progress may be gradual. Celebrate your achievements, no matter how small, and acknowledge the improvements you make along the way. Enjoy the process of learning and creating beautiful beadwork with each project you undertake.

CHAPTER 5

Beginner Project

Beaded Bracelet

- **Materials Needed:** Fabric (silk or cotton), tambour frame, tambour hook, embroidery or tambour thread beads (seed beads or small beads of your choice) clasp or closure.

- **Steps:**

  1. Stretch the fabric onto the tambour frame.

  2. Work a row of chain stitches along the edge of the fabric.

  3. Thread beads onto the tambour hook and attach them to the chain stitches, spacing them evenly.

  4. Continue adding rows of beads until you reach the desired length for your bracelet.

  5. Attach a clasp or closure to complete the bracelet.

Beaded Flower Brooch

• **Materials Needed:** Fabric (felt or silk), tambour frame, tambour hook, embroidery or tambour thread beads (various sizes and colors), brooch pin.

• **Steps:**

1. Stretch the fabric onto the tambour frame.

2. Draw or trace a simple flower shape onto the fabric.

3. Work chain stitches along the outline of the flower shape.

4. Fill in the petals with rows of beads, varying the colors and sizes for visual interest.

5. Add a center bead for the flower's stamen.

6. Attach a brooch pin to the back of the fabric to create a wearable brooch.

Beaded Bookmark

• **Materials Needed:** Fabric (satin or linen), tambour frame, tambour hook, embroidery or tambour thread, beads (seed beads or small beads of your choice), ribbon or tassel (optional)

- **Steps:**

  1. Stretch the fabric onto the tambour frame.

  2. Work a row of chain stitches along one edge of the fabric.

  3. Thread beads onto the tambour hook and attach them to the chain stitches, creating a decorative border.

  4. Add additional rows of beads or embroidery stitches to embellish the bookmark, experimenting with different patterns and motifs.

  5. Attach a ribbon or tassel to the top edge of the bookmark for a finishing touch.

Beaded Coin Purse

• **Materials Needed:** Fabric (satin or velvet), tambour frame, tambour hook, embroidery or tambour thread, beads (various sizes and colors), Zipper

- **Steps**:

  1. Stretch the fabric onto the tambour frame.

  2. Work a row of chain stitches around the perimeter of the fabric, leaving an opening for the zipper.

  3. Thread beads onto the tambour hook and attach them to the chain stitches, covering the entire surface of the coin purse.

  4. Add additional rows of beads or embroidery stitches to create patterns or designs.

  5. Attach the zipper to the opening of the coin purse to complete the project.

Beaded Hair Accessory

• **Materials Needed:** Fabric (silk or satin), tambour frame, tambour hook, embroidery or tambour thread, Beads (pearls, crystals, or decorative beads), hair comb or clip.

- **Steps:**

  1. Stretch the fabric onto the tambour frame.

  2. Work a row of chain stitches along the edge of the fabric, forming a decorative border.

  3. Thread beads onto the tambour hook and attach them to the chain stitches, creating a beaded trim.

  4. Create small beaded motifs such as flowers, leaves, or swirls to adorn the hair accessory.

  5. Attach the beaded fabric to a hair comb or clip to complete the accessory.

These beginner tambour beading projects offer a great way to practice basic techniques while creating beautiful and functional items. Experiment with different materials, colors, and bead arrangements to personalize each project according to your preferences.

INTERMEDIATE PROJECT

Beaded Clutch Purse

- **Materials Needed**: Fabric (satin or velvet), tambour frame, tambour hook, embroidery or tambour thread, beads (various sizes and colors), zipper or clasp, lining fabric

- **Steps:**

  1. Stretch the fabric onto the tambour frame.

  2. Work a dense pattern of chain stitches or other basic stitches over the entire surface of the fabric.

  3. Thread beads onto the tambour hook and attach them to the stitches, covering the fabric with intricate beadwork.

  4. Add additional embellishments such as sequins, pearls, or crystals to enhance the design.

5. Attach a zipper or clasp to the top edge of the fabric and sew lining fabric to the interior to complete the clutch purse.

Beaded Evening Shawl

- **Materials Needed:** Fabric (silk chiffon or organza), tambour frame, tambour hook, embroidery or tambour thread, beads (various sizes and colors, fringe trim (optional)

Steps:

1. Stretch the fabric onto the tambour frame.

2. Work a border of chain stitches or other decorative stitches around the edges of the fabric.

3. Create a dense pattern of tambour beading across the surface of the fabric, covering it with beads and sequins.

4. Experiment with different bead arrangements and motifs to create visual interest and texture.

5. Attach fringe trim to the edges of the shawl for added elegance and movement.

Beaded Statement Necklace

- **Materials Needed:** Fabric (satin or velvet), tambour frame, tambour hook, embroidery or tambour thread, beads (pearls, crystals, or decorative beads), ribbon or cord for necklace base

- **Steps:**

  1. Stretch the fabric onto the tambour frame.

  2. Work a row of chain stitches along the edge of the fabric, forming a base for the necklace.

  3. Create beaded motifs such as flowers, leaves, or geometric shapes using tambour beading techniques.

  4. Attach the beaded motifs to a ribbon or cord to create the necklace base.

5. Embellish the necklace with additional beads, sequins, or embroidery stitches as desired.

Beaded Decorative Pillow Cover

- **Materials Needed:** Fabric (cotton or linen), tambour frame, tambour hook, embroidery or tambour thread, beads (various sizes and colors), pillow insert

- **Steps:**

  1. Stretch the fabric onto the tambour frame.

  2. Work a border of chain stitches or other decorative stitches around the edges of the fabric.

  3. Create a central design or motif using tambour beading techniques, covering it with beads and sequins.

  4. Add additional embellishments such as embroidery stitches or appliqué to enhance the design.

  5. Sew the finished fabric onto a pillow cover or attach it to an

existing pillow cover to create a decorative accent for your home.

Beaded Bridal Veil

- **Materials Needed:** Fine tulle or organza fabric, ambour frame, tambour hook, embroidery or tambour thread, beads (pearls, crystals, or decorative beads), comb or headband for securing the veil.

- **Steps:**

  1. Stretch the fabric onto the tambour frame.

  2. Work a border of chain stitches or other decorative stitches around the edges of the fabric.

  3. Create a delicate pattern of tambour beading across the surface of the veil, focusing on the edges and corners.

  4. Embellish the design with clusters of beads, sequins, or embroidery stitches for added sparkle.

5. Attach the finished veil to a comb or headband to secure it in place for the bride's special day.

These intermediate tambour beading projects offer opportunities to explore more complex designs and techniques while creating beautiful and personalized items. Experiment with different materials, colors, and bead arrangements to customize each project according to your preferences and style.

CHAPTER 6

Advanced Project

Beaded Evening Gown

- **Materials Needed:** Silk or satin fabric, tambour frame tambour hook embroidery or tambour thread, beads (pearls, crystals, or decorative beads), sequins, lining fabric

- **Steps:**

  1. Stretch the fabric onto the tambour frame.

  2. Work a border of chain stitches or other decorative stitches along the neckline, hemline, and sleeve edges.

  3. Create intricate beadwork designs on the bodice, skirt, and sleeves using tambour beading techniques.

  4. Embellish the beadwork with sequins, pearls, or crystals to add sparkle and dimension.

5. Sew lining fabric to the interior of the gown to complete the garment.

Beaded Wall Hanging Tapestry

•**Materials Needed:** Linen or cotton fabric, tambour frame, tambour hook, embroidery or tambour thread,beads (various sizes and colors, sequins, wooden dowel or curtain rod

- **Steps:**

  1. Stretch the fabric onto the tambour frame.

  2. Work a border of chain stitches or other decorative stitches around the edges of the fabric.

  3. Create a central design or motif using tambour beading techniques, covering it with beads, sequins, and embroidery stitches.

  4. Fill in the background of the tapestry with additional beadwork or embroidery to add texture and interest.

5. Attach the finished fabric to a wooden dowel or curtain rod for hanging.

Beaded Bridal Tiara

- **Materials Needed:** Metal tiara base, tambour hook, embroidery or tambour thread beads (pearls, crystals, or decorative beads) sequins

- **Steps:**

  1. Remove any existing decoration from the metal tiara base.

  2. Stretch the fabric onto the tambour frame.

  3. Work a border of chain stitches or other decorative stitches along the edges of the fabric.

  4. Create intricate beadwork designs on the fabric, focusing on the front of the tiara where it will be most visible.

  5. Attach the beaded fabric to the metal tiara base using glue or stitching, ensuring it is securely fastened.

6. Embellish the beadwork with sequins, pearls, or crystals to add extra sparkle and dimension.

Beaded Statement Earrings

- **Materials Needed:** Fabric (silk or velvet), tambour frame, tambour hook, embroidery or tambour thread, beads (pearls, crystals, or decorative beads), tarring findings (hooks, studs, or clips)

- **Steps:**

  1. Stretch the fabric onto the tambour frame.

  2. Work a border of chain stitches or other decorative stitches along the edges of the fabric.

  3. Create intricate beadwork designs on the fabric, focusing on smaller motifs that will fit onto earring-sized pieces.

  4. Cut out the beaded fabric into earring shapes (circles, ovals, etc.).

5. Attach the beaded fabric to earring findings using glue or stitching, ensuring they are securely fastened.

Beaded Decorative Table Runner

- **Materials Needed:** Linen or cotton fabric, tambour frame, tambour hook, embroidery or tambour thread, beads (various sizes and colors), sequins

- **Steps:**

  - Stretch the fabric onto the tambour frame.

  - Work a border of chain stitches or other decorative stitches around the edges of the fabric.

  - Create a central design or motif using tambour beading techniques, covering it with beads, sequins, and embroidery stitches.

  - Extend the beadwork along the length of the table runner, filling in the background with additional beadwork or embroidery.

- Sew lining fabric to the back of the table runner to complete the project.

These advanced tambour beading projects offer opportunities to explore complex designs and techniques while creating stunning and intricate pieces. Experiment with different materials, colors, and bead arrangements to customize each project according to your preferences and style.

TROUBLESHOOTING AND SOLUTIONS

Troubleshooting is a crucial part of tambour beading, as it allows you to identify and address issues that may arise during the process. Beloew are some common problems encountered in tambour beading and their solutions:

1. Thread Tension Issues:

• **Problem:** Uneven or loose tension in the thread can result in sloppy stitches or fabric puckering.

• **Solution:** Adjust the tension of your tambour hook by gently tightening or loosening the screw mechanism. Practice with scrap fabric to find the optimal tension for your specific project. Additionally, make sure to maintain consistent tension as you work by applying even pressure on the tambour hook.

2. Beads Getting Stuck on the Hook:

• **Problem**: Beads may get stuck on the tambour hook, making it difficult to pull them through the fabric.

• **Solution:** Choose beads with smooth edges and holes that are slightly larger than the diameter of your tambour hook. If a bead gets stuck, gently wiggle the hook to loosen it or use a needle to help guide the bead through the fabric. Avoid forcing the bead, as this can damage both the bead and the fabric.

3. Fabric Snagging or Tearing:

• **Problem:** Fabric may snag or tear when working with the tambour hook, especially if it is stretched too tightly on the frame.

• **Solution:** Use a tambour frame that allows you to adjust the tension of the fabric without stretching it too tightly. Be gentle when inserting and pulling the tambour hook through the fabric, taking care to avoid catching or snagging the threads. If you encounter a snag, carefully trim any loose threads and reinforce the area with additional stitches if necessary.

4. Beads Falling Off:

• **Problem**: Beads may fall off the fabric after they have been attached, particularly if the thread tension is too loose or if the beads are not securely anchored.

• **Solution**: Ensure that the thread tension is tight enough to hold the beads securely in place without distorting the fabric. Use additional stitches or knots to secure beads, especially if they are large or heavy. Consider using a clear fabric glue or adhesive to reinforce bead attachments, particularly for items that will be subjected to frequent handling or movement.

5. Difficulty Creating Smooth Curves:

• **Problem:** Tambour beading requires precision when working around curves or intricate shapes, and it can be challenging to maintain smooth lines.

• **Solution:** Practice creating smooth curves by working slowly and deliberately, adjusting the angle of the tambour hook as needed. Use your non-dominant hand to guide the fabric and maintain even tension. Experiment with different stitching techniques, such as shortening or lengthening stitches, to achieve the desired curve.

6. Thread Breakage:

- **Problem:** Thread may break while working on a project, disrupting the continuity of the beadwork.

- **Solution:** Check for any sharp edges or rough spots on the tambour hook that may be causing the thread to fray or break. Use high-quality embroidery or tambour thread that is strong and durable. Avoid pulling the thread too tightly, as this can weaken it and increase the risk of breakage. If thread breakage occurs, tie off the broken ends with a knot and continue stitching with a fresh length of thread.

By addressing these common issues with tambour beading and implementing the suggested solutions, you can troubleshoot problems effectively and enjoy a smoother and more successful beadwork experience.

CHAPTER 7

Conclusion

In conclusion, tambour beading is a beautiful and intricate form of embellishment that allows for the creation of stunning and unique designs. From simple beginner projects to advanced masterpieces, tambour beading offers a wide range of creative possibilities for artisans of all skill levels. By mastering basic techniques and gradually exploring more complex methods, individuals can develop their tambour beading skills and create exquisite beadwork pieces.

Throughout this guide, we've explored the history, techniques, materials, and projects associated with tambour beading. We've covered everything from setting up the tambour frame to troubleshooting common issues encountered during the beadwork process. Whether you're interested in creating delicate jewelry pieces, elegant accessories, or ornate home décor items, tambour beading provides endless opportunities for artistic expression and craftsmanship.

As you embark on your tambour beading journey, remember to practice patience, attention to detail, and perseverance. Celebrate your progress and achievements along the way, and don't be afraid to experiment with new ideas and techniques. Whether you're a novice or an experienced beadwork artist, tambour beading offers a rewarding and fulfilling creative outlet that can inspire and delight both the maker and the viewer alike.

Printed in Great Britain
by Amazon

59924503R00060